NORTHUME

Wit & Humour

PERCY TWEED

BRADWELL
BOOKS

Published by Bradwell Books
9 Orgreave Close Sheffield S13 9NP
Email: books@bradwellbooks.co.uk
Compiled by Percy Tweed

British Library Cataloguing in Publication Data: a catalogue record for this book is
available from the British Library.

1st Edition
ISBN: 9781910551233

Print: Gomer Press, Llandysul, Ceredigion SA44 4JL
Design by: Jenks Design
Illustrations: ©Tim O'Brien 2015

At a primary school in Hexham the teacher came up with a good problem for her maths class to solve.

"Suppose, there were a dozen sheep and six of them jumped over a fence," she said to the group of seven-year-olds, "How many would be left?"

Little Harry, a farmer's son, put his hand up. "None," he answered.

"None?" exclaimed his teacher. "Harry, I'm afraid you don't know your arithmetic."

"Really, Miss?" said Harry, cockily, "And yee donnat knaa yer sheep. When one goes, they aal go!"

After seeing a documentary on how inner city youths can remove the wheels of cars in under four seconds with no specialist equipment, the McLaren team at Silverstone decided to fire their pit crew and hire four youths from Blyth. As most races are won or lost in the pit lane, McLaren thought their nimble young fingers would give the team an advantage. The first race came along and the car drove into the pits. The youths went to work swiftly but the McLaren team boss noticed a real problem. Not only had the youths replaced all four wheels within four seconds but in another 10 seconds they'd re-sprayed the car, changed the number and sold it to the Ferrari team.

A man walks into a pub in Blyth with a pork pie on his head. The barman asks, "Aalreet, man, why are you wearing a pork pie on yer head?"

The man replies, "It's a family tradition. We always wear pork pies on wor heads on Tuesday."

The barman says, "But its Wednesday."

Sheepishly, the man says, "Man, Ah must look like a real fool."

Insurance Assessor: "What gear were you in at the moment of the impact?"

Woman Driver: "Gucci sweats and Reeboks."

A gang of robbers broke into the Berwick-on-Tweed Lawyers' Club by mistake. The old legal lions put up a fierce fight for their lives and their money. The gang was happy to escape in one piece.

"It ain't so bad," one crook said. "At least we got fifty quid between us."

His boss screamed at him, "I warned you to stay clear of lawyers... we had 200 quid when we broke in!"

Two aerials meet on a roof, fall in love, get married. The ceremony was rubbish - but the reception was brilliant.

At a cricket match in Alnwick a fast bowler sent one down and it just clipped the bail. As nobody yelled "Ow's att", the batsman picked up the bail and replaced it. He looked at the umpire and said, "Windy the day, int it?"

"Aye," said the umpire, "Mind it doesn't blow yer cap off when you're walking back te the pavilion."

Many years ago, a miner fell down pit-shaft at Seghill Colliery. The deputy shouted, "Have yee broken owt, man?"

"Nae," called back the miner, "There's nowt te break doon here, just a few rocks!"

A lad from Wansbeck who had just started his first term at Durham University asked a third year, "Can you tell me where the library's at?"

The older student said disdainfully, "At the University of Durham we never end a sentence with a preposition."

The new boy tried again, "Can you tell me where the library's at, you wassock?"

Two hawks were sitting on their perch at Kielder Water Bird of Prey Centre.

"Look at that speed!" one hawk said to the other as a jet fighter plane roared over their heads on its way to RAF Spadeadam in Cumbria.

"Hmph!" snorted the second hawk. "You would fly fast too if your tail was on fire!"

A Northumbrian man is driving through County Durham when he passes a farmer standing in the middle of a huge field. He pulls the car over and watches the farmer standing stock-still, doing absolutely nothing. Intrigued, the man walks over to the farmer and asks him, "Excuse me, sir, but what are yee doing?"

The farmer replies, "Aas trying to win Nobel Prize."

"How?" Asks the puzzled Northumbrian man.

"Well," says the farmer, "Ah heard they give the prize to folk who are outstanding in their field."

A harried man runs into his GP's surgery in Wark.

"Doctor! Doctor! Me wife's in labour! But she keeps screaming, 'Shouldn't, couldn't, wouldn't, can't!'"

"Oh, that's okay," says the doctor. "She's just having contractions."

In a friendly match, Prudhoe Town beat Workington A.F.C. five – nothing; they were lucky to get nothing.

Supporters, waiting to watch Morpeth Town play Durham City A.F.C heard that the players from County Durham were going to be delayed.

They saw a sign on the A1 that said "Clean Lavatories"... so they did.

A passenger in a taxi tapped the driver on the shoulder to ask him something.

The driver screamed, lost control of the cab, nearly hit a bus, drove up over the curb and stopped just inches from a large plate glass window.

For a few moments everything was silent in the cab, then the driver said, "Please, don't ever do that again. You scared the daylights out of me."

The passenger, who was also frightened, apologised and said he didn't realise that a tap on the shoulder could frighten him so much, to which the driver replied, "I'm sorry, it's really not your fault at all. Today is my first day driving a cab. I've been driving a hearse for the last twenty-five years."

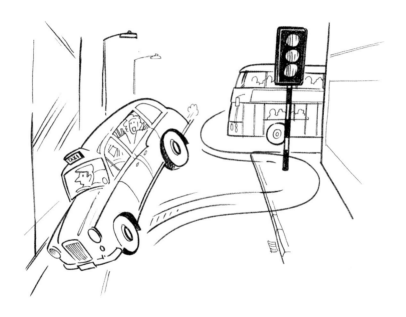

A group of backpackers from University of Northumbria were sitting around a campfire one evening when a stranger asked to join them. Glad to add to their group, they agreed. The evening's fun soon turned to jokes. One of the students started to tell jokes about how posh and lacking in common sense Durham University students were. The stranger who, it turned out, had graduated from Durham University himself, became more and more furious with each quip. Finally, he had had enough and pulled out his razor and began to threaten the Northumbrian lads with it. Fortunately for them, he couldn't find a socket to plug it into.

A plain Jane from Widdrington goes to see Madame Grizelda, a fortune-teller, and asks about her future love life.

Madame Grizelda tells her, "Two men are madly in love with you – Mark and Maurice."

"Who will be the lucky one?" asks Jane excitedly.

Madame Grizelda answers, "Maurice will marry you, and Mark will be the lucky one."

There's a man in Kendal who claims to have invented a game that's a bit like cricket; what he doesn't realise is Cumberland County Cricket Club's been playing it for years.

"You're looking glum," the captain of Bedlington C.C. remarked to one of his players.

"Yes, the doctor says I can't play cricket," said the downcast man.

"Really?" replied the captain, "I didn't know he'd ever seen you play?"

Psychiatrist: "What's your problem?"
Patient: "I think I'm a chicken."
Psychiatrist: "How long has this been going on?"
Patient: "Ever since I was an egg!"

A man from Rothbury decided to become a monk so he went to the monastery and talked to the head monk.

The head monk said, "You must take a vow of silence and can only say two words every three years."

The man agreed and after the first three years, the head monk came to him and said, "What are your two words?"

"Food cold!" the man replied.

Three more years went by and the head monk came to him and said, "What are your two words?" "Robe dirty!" the man exclaimed.

Three more years went by and the head monk came to him and said, "What are your two words?"

"I quit!" said the man. "Well," the head monk replied, "I'm not surprised. You've done nothing but complain ever since you got here!"

Q: What do you call a County Durham bloke in the 4th Round of the FA Cup?
A: The Referee.

Two Ashington Cricket Club players are chatting in the bar after a match. "So did you have a hard time explaining last week's game to the missus?" says one.

"I certainly did," says the other," She found out I wasn't there!"

An Amble man fell out with his in-laws and banned them from entering the house while he was in it. His wife faithfully carried out his wishes until she was on her death bed and then asked sadly, "Haven't I always been a supportive wife to you, John?"

"Aye, pet," he replied, "The best."

"Then I would love it if you could grant me last request and let me sister Sarah ride in the first car with you at me funeral?"

"Alreet, pet," he agreed heavily, "But I'm warning you, it'll spoil all me pleasure!"

Two blokes are standing in the Morpeth Job Centre, waiting for their turn at the counter.

The first bloke says to the second one, "Ah have te buy me missus summat nice for our wedding anniversary and the benefits cheque willn't cover it."

The second bloke looks up from his paper and says, "What date?" The first bloke thinks for a while and says, "15th September."
The second bloke considers his next question. "What year?"

Without taking a breath, the first bloke replies, "Every year for the last twenty-seven!

A council trainee on a site in Berwick-on-Tweed is surveying the land about to be dug up.

The gaffer says to him, "Yee gan and get the metal detector and check for pipe work, man, and I'll get the kettle on and have a mash."

The gaffer gets the tea going while his trainee starts work. Half-hour later the gaffer puts his paper down, next to his mug of tea, to find out how work is progressing and he finds the lad sitting on a wall scratching his head.

"What's up with yee, man?" The gaffer asks. "There's pipework all over the place. Look!"

The young worker sets off across the land, the bleeper sounding continuously as the detector passes in front of him.

The gaffer watches him, laughing, then he says, "Are yee soft or what, man? You've got steel toe caps in yer boots!"

Down the Miners' Arms, a group of blokes sit around drinking when a mobile phone on the table rings. One of the men picks up the mobile and puts the speaker-phone on.

A woman's voice says, "How are you, darling? I hope you don't mind but I've just seen a diamond ring priced £2000 and wondered if I can buy it? I've got your credit card with me."

"Of course, pet, go ahead," answers the man.

"While I'm on," purrs the lady, "I've noticed a top of the range car I'd like. It's only £65,000, could I order that as well?"

"Of course, hinny," replies the man.

His friends around the table look at each other in disbelief as the lady continues, "And I've just noticed a house in Corbridge, man. It's only £750,000 - could we have that as well please?"

"Of course, poppet," answers the man, without so much as blinking.

The phone call is ended and the man smiles at the others and takes a long swill of beer. Then he looks around and shouts "Anyone knaa whose phone this is?"

It was match day for Prudhoe Town F.C. and excited crowds filled the streets, heading for the Kimberley Park stadium. A funeral procession drove slowly through the throng. One of the Citizens supporters stopped, took off his hat and bowed reverently as the hearse passed.

"That was a nice thing to do," remarked his mate.

"Well," said the Citizens fan, "She was a good wife to me for thirty odd years."

Four University of Northumbria students taking their chemistry degree had done very well in their exams so far. Because of this, even though their last exam of the year was fast approaching, the four friends decided to go back to their hometown of Berwick-on-Tweed and catch up with some friends there. They had a great time partying.

However, after all the fun, they slept all day on Sunday and didn't make it back to the university until early Monday morning which was the time of their final exam. Rather than taking the exam, they decided to find their professor after it was over and explain to him why they missed it. They told him that they had gone home to do some studying for the weekend and had planned to come back in time for the exam.

But unfortunately, they had a flat tyre on the way back, didn't have a spare, and couldn't get help for a long time. As a result, they had only just arrived!

The professor thought it over and then agreed they could make up their final exam the following day. The four were very relieved. They studied hard that night – all night – and went in the next day at the time the professor had told them. He placed them in separate rooms and handed each of them a test booklet and told them to begin.

The first problem was worth five points. It was something simple about a specific chemistry topic. "Great," they all thought, "This is going to be easy." They each finished the problem and turned the page. On the second page was written, "Question 2 (for 95 points): Which tyre?"

"Dad," says the little boy," Can Ah play footie with the lads in the street?"

"Nae,"says his dad,"They swear tee much."

"But yee play with them, Dad?"

"Ah swear already."

Derek and Duncan were long-time neighbours in Wooler. Every time, Derek saw Duncan coming round to his house, his heart sank. This was because he knew that, as always, Duncan would be visiting him in order to borrow something and he was fed up with it.

"I'm not going to let Duncan get away with it this time," he said quietly to his wife, "Watch what I'm about to do."

"Hi there, I wondered if you were thinking about using your hedge trimmer this afternoon?" asked Duncan.

"Oh, I'm very sorry," said Derek, trying to look apologetic, "but I'm actually going to be using it all afternoon."

"In that case," replied Duncan with a big grin, "You won't be using your golf clubs, will you? Mind if I borrow them?"

Three Berwick-on-Tweed women are talking in a bar about a party they've been invited to.

The first one says, "We've got to all wear an item that matches something belonging to our husbands at this party, haven't we?"

"Yeah," said the other two, "But what?"

The first one continued, "Well, my husband's got black hair and I've got a little black dress I can diet into by then."

The second one says, "That's a good idea. My husband has got brown hair and I've got a brown dress I can diet into by then too."

The third one looks a bit hesitant and says, "I just need to go on a diet - my husband's bald!"

A lawyer at Magistrates Court in Bedlington says to the chair of the bench, "Your worship, I wish to appeal my client's case on the basis of newly discovered evidence."

The magistrate replied, "And what is the nature of the new evidence?"

The lawyer says, "Your worship, I discovered that my client still has £500 left."

Darren proudly drove his new convertible into Berwick-on-Tweed and parked it on the main street. He was on his way to the recycling centre to get rid of an unwanted gift, a foot spa, which he left on the back seat.

He had walked half way down the street when he realised that he had left the top down with the foot spa still in the back.

He ran all the way back to his car, but it was too late...another five foot spas had been dumped in the car.

Ten women out on a hen night in Blyth thought it would be sensible if one of them stayed more sober than the other nine and looked after the money to pay for their drinks. After deciding who would hold the money, they all put twenty pounds into the kitty to cover expenses. At closing time after a few wine spritzers, several vodka and cokes, and a Pina Colada each, they stood around deciding how to divvy up the leftover cash.

"How do we stand?" said Sharon.

"Stand?!" said Debbie. "That's the easy part! I'm wondering how I can walk. I've missed the last bus to Seaton Sluice!"

A man rushed into Hexham General Hospital and asked a nurse for a cure for hiccups. Grabbing a cup of water, the nurse quickly splashed it into the man's face.

"What did yer do that for?" screamed the man, wiping his face.

"Well, you don't have the hiccups now, do you?" said the nurse.

"Nae," replied the man. "But me missus oot in the car does.

Q: What's the difference between Durham City A.F.C. and a teabag?

A: A teabag stays in the cup a lot longer.

One afternoon at the University of Northumbria, a group of freshers, who had just started their psychology course, were attending one of their first seminars. The topic was emotional extremes.

"Let's begin by discussing some contrasts," said the tutor. He pointed to a student in the front row, "What is the opposite of joy?"

The student thought about it briefly, then answered "Sadness." The tutor asked another student, "What is the opposite of depression?"

She paused then said, "Elation."

"And you," the tutor said to another student sitting at the back, "What about the opposite of woe?"

The student thought for a moment, then replied, "Um, I believe that would be 'giddy up'."

A man went into a butcher's shop in Alnwick and said, "Excuse me, do you have a sheep's head?"

The Butcher replied, "Nae, it's just a very tight perm."

One Sunday in Our Lady and St. Cuthbert's church, Prudhoe, the vicar opened his Bible and began to read the lesson. In a loud voice, he proclaimed, "Corinthians 7."

A keen Citizens fan, who had been dozing in the front pew, woke up with a start and shouted out, "Blimey! Who were they playing?"

A farmer in Powburn says to his friend, "I can't decide whether to buy a bicycle or a new cow."

His friend replies, "You'd look pretty silly riding a cow."

"I'd look even sillier trying to milk a bicycle," retorts the farmer.

In a school in Wansbeck, a little boy just wasn't getting good marks. One day, his teacher was checking his homework and said, "Lee, once again I'm afraid I can only give you two out of ten."

Little Lee looked up at her and said, "Well, Miss, Ah don't want to scare you, but…"

He stopped, a worried expression on his face.

"What is it? Tell me, Lee," said his teacher kindly.

"Well," said the boy, "me daddy says if ah divvent get betta marks soon, somebody is gunna get a spanking."

A police officer arrived at the scene of a major pile up on the A68.

The officer runs over to the front car and asks the driver, "Are you seriously hurt?"

The driver turns to the officer and says, "How the heck should I know? Do I look like a lawyer?"

Man: "My wife went swimming in the river Tweed."
His mate: "Coldstream?"
Man: "Yeah, she said it was quite chilly."

A lad from Blyth went for a job interview. It was going quite well until the interviewer handed him a laptop and said, "Sell this to me." So the lad put it under his arm, left the interview and went home. Half an hour later his prospective employer phoned demanding the return of the laptop. "Aalreet, man," says the lad from Blyth, "five hundred quid and it's yours."

Q: Why was the sheep arrested on the A1?

A: She did a ewe-turn

An old bloke at the bus stop outside Wansbeck Hospital is talking to the next person in the queue whilst rubbing his head.

"Me wooden leg in't half giving me some gyp," complained the old boy.

The person in the queue looks at him, wondering why he keeps rubbing his head, and says, "Really? Why?"

The old man retorted, "Cos me missus keeps hitting me over the head with it!"

A policeman stops a man in a car in the middle of Cramlington with a sheep in the front seat.

"What are you doing with that sheep, man?" He asks. "You should take it to a zoo."

The following week, the same policeman sees the same man again with the sheep in the front seat of the car. Both of them are wearing sunglasses. The policeman pulls him over. "I thought you were going to take that sheep to the zoo?"

The man replies, "I did. We had such a good time we are going to Newbiggin-by-the-Sea this weekend!"

Sam worked in a telephone marketing company in Berwick-on-Tweed. One day he walked into his boss's office and said, "I'll be honest with you, I know the economy isn't great, but I have three companies after me, and, with respect, I would like to ask for a pay rise."

After a few minutes of haggling, his manager finally agreed to a 5% pay rise, and Sam happily got up to leave.

"By the way," asked the boss as Sam went to the door, "Which three companies are after you?"

"The electric company, the water company, and the phone company," Sam replied.

A farmer was driving along a country road near the village of Netherton Burtfoot with a large load of fertiliser. A little boy, playing in front of his cottage, saw him and called out, "What do you have on your truck?"

"Fertiliser," the farmer replied.

"What are you going to do with it?" asked the little boy.

"Put it on strawberries," answered the farmer.

"You ought to live here," the little boy advised him. "We put sugar and cream on ours."

It was a quiet night in Harbottle and a man and his wife were fast asleep, when there was an unexpected knock on the door. The man looked at his alarm clock. It was half past three in the morning. "I'm not getting out of bed at this time," he thought and rolled over.

There was another louder knock.

"Aren't you going to answer that?" asked his wife irritably.

So the man dragged himself out of bed and went downstairs. He opened the door to find a strange man standing outside. It didn't take the homeowner long to realise the man was totally drunk.

"Aalreet, man," slurred the stranger. "Can yee gissus a push?"

"No, I'm sorry I most certainly can't. It's half past three in the morning and I was in bed," said the man and he slammed the front door.

He went back up to bed and told his wife what happened. "That wasn't very nice of you," she said. "Remember that night we broke down in the pouring rain on the way to pick the kids up from the babysitter, and you had to knock on that man's door to get us started again? What would have happened if he'd told us to get lost?"

"But the man who just knocked on our door was lashed," replied her husband.

"Well, we can at least help move his car somewhere safe and sort him out a taxi," said his wife. "He needs our help."

So the husband got out of bed again, got dressed, and went downstairs. He opened the door, but couldn't to see the stranger anywhere so he shouted, "Hey, do you still want a push?"

In answer, he heard a voice call out, "Aye, man, please!"

So, still unable to see the stranger, he shouted, "Where are you?"
"Ahm o'er here, man," the stranger replied, "on yer swing."

A lady from Morpeth walks past a pet shop every day on her way to work. One day she notices a parrot and stops to admire the bird. The parrot says to her, "Aal reet, pet? Yee are a geet big ugly lass."

Well, the lady is furious! She storms off but, on her way back from work, she passes the same parrot and, when it sees her, the bird says, "Aal reet, pet? Yee are a geet big ugly lass."

She is incredibly angry now so she goes to the manager and threatens to sue the pet shop. She demands to have the bird put down. The manager apologises profusely and promises that the bird won't say it again. The next day, she decides to go back and check. She walks past the parrot and, when it sees her, it says, "Aal reet, pet?"

The woman stops, scowls and with an icy stare, says, "Yes?"

The parrot struts back and forth on its perch in a cocky manner, gawping at her, then it says, "Yee knaa."

A pupil at a school in Chatton asked his teacher, "Are 'trousers' singular or plural?"

The teacher replied, "They're singular on top and plural on the bottom."

The president of the Berwick-on-Tweed Vegetarian Society really couldn't control himself any more. He simply had to try some pork, just to see what it tasted like. So one day he told his members he was going away for a short break. He left town and headed to a restaurant in a country house hotel on the border. He sat down, ordered a roasted pig, and waited impatiently for his treat. After only a few minutes, he heard someone call his name, and, to his horror, he saw one of his members walking towards him. At exactly the same moment, the waiter arrived at his table, with a huge platter, holding a whole roasted pig with an apple in its mouth. "Isn't this place something?" said the president, thinking quickly, "Look at the way they serve apples!"

Phil's nephew came to him with a problem. "I have my choice of two women," he said, with a worried frown, "A beautiful, penniless young girl whom I love dearly, and a rich widow who I don't really love."

"Follow your heart," Phil counselled, "marry the lass you love." "Very well, Uncle Phil," said the nephew, "That's sound advice. Thank you."

"You're welcome," replied Phil with a smile, "By the way, where does the widow live?"

Have you heard about the latest machine in the arcade in Berwick-on-Tweed town centre?

You put ten pence in and ask it any question and it gives you a true answer. One visitor from Durham tried it last week.

He asked the machine "Where is my father?" The machine replied: "Your father is fishing on the River Derwent."
"Well," he thought, "That's daft for a start because my father is dead."

Next he asked, "Where is my mother's husband?" The reply came back, "Your mother's husband is buried in Darlington, but your father is still fishing on the River Derwent."

A farmer from Keswick in the Lake District once visited a farmer based near Berwick-on-Tweed. The visitor asked, "How big is yewer farm?" to which the Berwick-on-Tweed farmer replied, "Can yee see those trees over there? That's the boundary of me farmland".

"Is that all, man?" said the Cumbrian farmer, "It takes us three days to drive to the boundary of ma farm."

The Berwick-on-Tweed man looked at him and said, "Ah had a car like that once."

The nervous young batsman playing for South Northumberland C.C. was having a very bad day. In a quiet moment in the game, he muttered to the one of his team mates, "Well, I suppose you've seen worse players.""

There was no response...so he said it again, "I said 'I guess you've seen worse players'."

His team mate looked at him and answered, "I heard you the first time. I was just trying to think..."

Man: "I went to Hexham and had a terrible cup of tea."
His Mate: "Once Brewed?"
Man: "Yes, but too much milk."

One day at Wansbeck hospital, a group of primary school children were being given a tour. A nurse showed them the x-ray machines and asked them if they had ever had broke a bone.

One little boy raised his hand, "I did!"

"Did it hurt?" the nurse asked.

"Nae!" he replied.

"Wow, you must be a very brave boy!" said the nurse. "What did you break?"

"Me sister's arm!"

A woman from Morpeth called Mandy was still not married at thirty-five and she was getting really tired of going to family weddings especially because her old Aunt Maud always came over and said, "You're next!"

It made Mandy so annoyed she racked her brains to figure out how to get Aunt Maud to stop. Sadly, an old uncle died and there was a big family funeral. Mandy spotted Aunt Maud in the crematorium, walked over, pointed at the coffin and said, with a big smile, "You're next!"

For a minute Workington A.F.C. were in with a chance – then the game started.

At a school in Blyth, the maths teacher poses a question to little Wayne, "If I give £500 to your dad on 12% interest per annum, what will I get back after two years."

"Nowt," says Wayne.

"I am afraid you know nothing about maths, Wayne," says the teacher crossly.

"Ah'm afraid too, sir," replies Wayne, "Yee divint know nowt about me father."

When the manager of Carlisle United F.C. started to tell the team about tactics, half the players thought he was talking about a new kind of peppermint.

A Hexham man and his wife are walking past Josephine's restaurant at Langley Castle when some delicious aromas waft towards them. "Did you smell that food?" the woman asked. "Wonderful!"

Being the kind-hearted, generous man that he was, her husband thought, "What the heck, I'll treat her!" So they walked past it a second time.

Albert, an extremely wealthy 65 year-old, arrives at Dunstanburgh Castle Golf Club in Embleton with a beautiful 25-year-old blonde on his arm.

His buddies at the club are all aghast. They corner him and ask, "Albert, how did you get the trophy girlfriend?"

"Girlfriend!" exclaims, Albert, "She's me missus!" His friends are shocked, but continue to ask, "So, how'd you persuade her to marry you?" Albert replies, "I lied about me age."

His friends respond, "What do you mean? Did you tell her you were only 50?"

Albert smiles and says, "No, I told her I was 81."

An expectant father rang the Hillcrest Maternity Unit in Alnwick to see how his wife, who had gone into labour, was getting on. By mistake, he was connected to the county cricket ground in Jesmond.

"How's it going?" he asked.

"Fine," came the answer, "We've got three out and hope to have the rest out before lunch. The last one was a duck."

What do you get if you cross the Durham City A. F.C. with an OXO cube?
A laughing stock.

Did you hear about the last wish of the henpecked husband of a house-proud wife?

He asked to have his ashes scattered on the carpet.

A golfer was going around the Bamburgh Castle Golf Club course. He was talking to his caddy between holes about a forthcoming competition. "I've been drawn against Jack Smith from Carlisle, is he any good?"

The caddy checked for a moment and said, "He's absolutely rubbish. Can't get around the course with any ease. He set a new course record for the worst round ever that has only just been beaten."

"Oh, I should easily get through to the next round then, shan't I?" said the golfer complacently.

The caddy looked down at the scorecard and said, "I wouldn't bet on it!"

Three blondes were walking in Cockley Burn Wood when they came upon a set of tracks.

The first blonde said, "Those are deer tracks."

The second blonde said, "No, those are horse tracks."

The third blonde said, "You're both wrong, those are cattle tracks."

The Blondes were still arguing when the 11.45 train to Berwick-on-Tweed hit them.

Pete and Larry hadn't seen each other in many years. They were having a long chat, telling each other all about their lives. Finally Pete invited Larry to visit him in his new flat in Morpeth. "I have a wife and three kids and I'd love to have you visit us." "Great. Where do you live?"

"Here's the address. There's plenty of parking behind the flat. Park and come around to the front door, kick it open with your foot, go to the lift and press the button with your left elbow, then enter! When you reach the sixth floor, go down the hall until you see my name on the door. Then press the doorbell with your right elbow and I'll let you in."

"Great. But tell me...what is all this business of kicking the front door open, then pressing elevator buttons with my right, then my left elbow?" Pete answered, "Surely you're not coming empty-handed?"

Anne and Matt, a couple from Alnwick, went to the Northumberland County Show and found a weighing scale that tells your fortune and weight.

"Hey, listen to this," said Matt, showing his wife a small white card. "It says I'm bright, energetic, and a great husband."

"Aye," Anna said, "And it has your weight wrong as well."

A Hurrah Henry from Kendal was driving around Morpeth in his fancy new car and realised that he was lost. The driver stopped a local character, old Tom, and said, "Hey, you there! Old man, what happens if I turn left here?"

"Ah divvent knaa, man," replied Tom. "Well, what if I turn right here - where will that take me?" continued the visitor.

"Ah divvent knaa, man," replied old Tom.   Becoming exasperated, the driver continued, "Well, what if I go straight on?"
A flicker of knowledge passed over old Tom's face but then he replied, "Ah divvent knaa, man."

"I say, old man, you don't know a lot do you?" retorted the posh bloke.

Old Tom looked at him and said, "Ah may not know a lot, man, but Ah ain't lost like what yee are!" With that, old Tom walked off leaving the motorist stranded.

Three sisters aged 92, 94 and 96 live in a house together in Ulgham. One night the 96 year-old draws a bath. She puts her foot in and pauses. She yells to the other sisters, "Were Ah getting in or out of the bath, pet?"

The 94 year-old hollers back, "Ah divvent knaa. Ah'll come up and see."

She starts up the stairs but then she pauses, "Were Ah going upstairs or down, pet?"

The 92 year-old is sitting at the kitchen table having tea listening to her sisters. She shakes her head and says, "Ah hope Ah never get that forgetful, knock on wood." She raps on the oak table loudly. Then she shouts upstairs, "A'll come up and help the pair of yee as soon as Ah see who's at the door."

A labourer in Stannington shouted up to his roofer mate on top of an old terraced house, saying, "Divn't start climbing down this ladder, Bert."

"Why not?" Bert called back.

"Cos Ah moved it five minutes ago, man!' replied his mate.

A bloke walked up to the foreman of a road laying gang in Ponteland and asked for a job. "Ah got nowt for you today, lad," said the foreman, looking up from his newspaper. "But if you walk half a mile down there, you will find the gang and you can see if you like the work. Ah can put you on the list for tomorrow."

"That's canny, man," said the bloke as he wandered off down the road.

At the end of the shift, the man walked past the foreman and shouted, "Thanks, man. See you in the morning."
The foreman looked up from his paper and called back, "You've enjoyed yersel' then, lad?"

"Aye, Ah 'ave, man!" the bloke shouted, "But can Ah 'ave a shovel or a pick te lean on like the rest of the gang tomorrow?"

In the staff canteen, Jack was always showing Bob photos of his dog and saying how clever it was: doing tricks, playing ball, bringing his newspaper and slippers. One day Jack brought in the album from his daughter's wedding so Bob could look through the photos. Bob decided to tease Jack a little and said, "Hang on, where's yee precious dog? Ah'm surprised he wasn't the Best Man!"

Jack looked at Bob as if he was stupid, "Divvent be foolish, someone had to take the photos."

There were two caterpillars on a leaf, a butterfly flies past and one says to the other, "You'll never get me up in one of them."